P9-CCC-742

# ENDANGERED ANIMALS

## by Megan Stine

A TRUMPET CLUB ORIGINAL BOOK

Published by The Trumpet Club, Inc.,
a subsidiary of Bantam Doubleday Dell Publishing Group, Inc.,
1540 Broadway, New York, New York 10036.

ISBN 0-440-83025-7

Printed in the United States of America
September 1994
1   3   5   7   9   10   8   6   4   2
CWO

## PHOTOGRAPH CREDITS

*p.11:* © 1993 Comstock, Inc./Russ Kinne; *p. 13:* © Allan D. Cruickshank, National
Audubon Society/Photoresearchers, Inc.; *p. 23:* Patrick Martin-Vegue/Tom Stack
& Associates; *p. 24:* © Gerard Lacz/Peter Arnold, Inc.; *p. 30:* © 1985 James T.
Spencer/Photoresearchers, Inc.; *p. 37:* © Jen and Des Bartlett/Photoresearchers,
Inc.; *p. 41:* © Leonard Lee Rue III/Photoresearchers, Inc.; *p. 44:* © 1976 A. W.
Ambler, National Audubon Society/Photoresearchers, Inc.; *p. 47:* © 1973 Terence
O. Mathews/Photoresearchers, Inc.; *p. 50:* © Jeff Apoian/Photoresearchers, Inc.;
*p. 52:* © Carl D. Kolord, National Audubon Society/Photoresearchers, Inc.; *p. 54:*
Roy Toft/Tom Stack & Associates

*Cover:* Komodo dragon: © 1993 Comstock, Inc./Boyd Norton; Black rhinoceros:
Frans Lanting/Minden Pictures; California condor: © Peter B. Kaplan/
Photoresearchers, Inc.

# Contents

# Introduction

One day in 1813, John James Audubon stepped outside to see why the sky above his Ohio home was so dark. He looked up and saw an enormous flock of passenger pigeons. These birds got their name because they traveled over long distances, like passengers. There were so many of the birds that they blocked out the sun—for three days! Audubon guessed that a billion birds had passed over his house every few hours.

Audubon was a famous artist and bird expert. He loved birds, and devoted his life to studying and painting them. But he also hunted them. In those days, many people hunted birds, including passenger pigeons, partly for food and partly for sport. Almost no one imagined that passenger pigeons could become *extinct,* or die out completely.

Passenger pigeons were the most numerous birds that ever existed. They lived only in North America, in the East and Midwest. There were so many passenger pigeons that when they roosted in trees, the limbs broke from their weight. Sometimes whole trees fell over. When a hunter fired a single shot into a flock of a million birds, the shot could kill 70 pigeons at once!

To people living in the 1800s, it seemed as if passenger pigeons would be around forever. But just a little more than 100 years after Audubon saw billions of birds in one flock, the passenger pigeon was extinct. The last one died in the Cincinnati Zoo in 1914.

How was it possible for so many passenger pigeons to become extinct? There are two reasons. One is that too many pigeons were killed by human beings. The other is that their *habitat*—the place that has everything an animal needs to live and grow—was destroyed.

People don't destroy an animal's habitat on purpose. But it happens—sometimes by accident and sometimes because the human population grows, leaving less room for animals. Trees are cut down to make room for houses or towns, and the animals that live in the forest must find new homes. Fields are plowed so that crops can be planted. Then the field animals must also move.

Sometimes beaches are ruined when houses and hotels are built too close to the water. The buildings can destroy the sand dunes. Piers and jetties—walls that extend from the land into the water to help control the tides—can cause the beach itself to wash away. The sea creatures then can be damaged.

Some of these changes are a part of progress. But for wildlife, the changes mean that there is less natural space for birds and animals to live in.

This kind of progress is exactly what destroyed the passenger pigeon. The thick forests of Ohio, Kentucky, and Indiana were cut down in the 1800s to make room for American settlers. At the time, settlers didn't realize that passenger pigeons needed these trees to nest and feed.

And no one realized something else: There was a limit to how many passenger pigeons could be killed and still have the flock survive. When so many birds were shot, the flocks became too small. Passenger pigeons needed large flocks in order to mate. In small flocks, the pigeons didn't breed.

There are similar stories for all the animals you will read about in this book. Either their habitat has been destroyed or they have been hunted too much—or both. But one thing is different. Now we understand how we have endangered the lives of these animals. And knowing that, we can help save them.

Saving threatened animals takes unique efforts by very dedicated people. The whooping crane, tiger, sea turtle, Komodo dragon, rhinoceros, and California condor—the animals you will read about—are all endangered. But they have something else in common. They all have special stories about the extraordinary ways people are trying to save them. There are stories like these behind threatened animals all over the world. And once the stories are told, people everywhere, including you, can take steps to make sure that these wonderful animals are no longer endangered.

### What Is an Endangered Animal?

An endangered animal is one that is in danger of becoming extinct. When that happens, the animal is put on the Endangered Species List. This list is published by a government office called the U.S. Fish and

Wildlife Service. The list alone is a whole book. It is 36 pages long!

But who decides when an animal is endangered and should be put on the list? Lots of people do. Anyone can *nominate,* or suggest, an animal for the list, as long as they also present information about why it is endangered. Then expert scientists are asked to review the information and make a recommendation. If the U.S. Fish and Wildlife Service agrees with the experts' recommendations, the *species* is listed. (A species is a particular kind of plant or animal. For instance, a white rhinoceros is one species of rhinoceros.)

One way that experts decide whether an animal is endangered is to count the number of them remaining in the wild. If the number goes down steadily over a period of years, it's a signal that says HELP! The animal is in trouble and may soon become extinct.

Some animals are put on the list even though there are thousands of them left in the wild. For instance, there are about 5,000 tigers in India today—not a small number when taken by itself. But just 100 years ago, there were 50,000—ten times as many.

And not all animals exist in large numbers to begin with. For instance, scientists suspect that there were never more than a few thousand whooping cranes in America. That's quite a different number from the billions of passenger pigeons that once lived. So some species can become endangered more quickly, even if only a small number of them die out.

Today there are more than 1,200 animals—including mammals, fish, birds, reptiles, and amphibians—on the Endangered Species List. And animals are becoming endangered or extinct much faster than ever before. If you include plants and insects with the animals, almost 100 different species become extinct each year!

## The Magic Number

What is the most endangered animal? There isn't only one right answer to that question, although you might say that the California condor is one of the most endangered. Today there are only a few condors living in the wild, and they are not able to exist entirely on their own. But many other animals are also close to extinction. There are perhaps only a handful of sun bears, only a few dozen Javan rhinos, and only a few hundred pandas alive anywhere in the world today.

A few hundred pandas may not seem such a small number, but scientists believe that for a species to survive, there must be at least 250 animals remaining. When it comes to extinction, the magic number is 250. Here's why. With fewer than 250 animals remaining, a species can easily become too *inbred*. This means that because there are fewer animals to choose from, each animal will have a greater chance of mating with one of its cousins or other relatives. When that happens, all the offspring have the same family traits—including all the weaknesses—that the parents had. Weak traits are then passed along from one generation to the next, and the species is not as likely to survive.

Fortunately, there is something that scientists can do to help. They can breed endangered animals in zoos to make sure that their mates are carefully chosen. A tiger from one family can be mated with a tiger from a completely different family. This way their cubs will be more likely to have a good mixture of genes.

Breeding in zoos is called *captive breeding*. It is just one of the ways scientists are trying to help save endangered species. But captive breeding doesn't always work. Sometimes the animals refuse to mate in zoos. Still, you will be amazed when you learn how scientists are managing to help the animals breed—and how sneaky the scientists sometimes have to be!

### Endangered Animals: A Partial List

It would be impossible to list all the endangered animals here. There are too many of them. There are 20 species of endangered monkeys alone. But here is a partial listing of endangered animals throughout the world. When you see a plus sign (+) by the name, it means there are various species of the animal that are endangered. An asterisk (*) means that at least one species of the animal lives in North America.

*Alligator+ **
*Albatross, short-tailed*
*Antelope, giant sable*
*Armadillo+*
*Baboon, gelada*
*Bandicoot+*
*Bat+ **
*Bear+ **
*Bobcat*
*Caribou**
*Cheetah*
*Chimpanzee*
*Chinchilla*
*Condor, Andean*

*Condor, California**
*Cougar**
*Crane*[+] *
*Crocodile*[+] *
*Deer*[+] *
*Dolphin*[+]
*Eagle, bald**
*Elephant*[+]
*Falcon*[+] *
*Ferret, black-footed**
*Fox*[+] *
*Gazelle*[+]
*Gecko*[+]
*Gorilla*
*Hawk*[+] *
*Hog, pygmy*
*Horse, Przewalski's*
*Hyena*[+]
*Iguana*[+]
*Jaguar*
*Kangaroo*[+]
*Lemur*[+]
*Leopard*[+]
*Lion*[+]
*Macaque*[+]
*Macaw*[+]
*Manatee*[+] *
*Monitor*[+]
*Monkey*[+]
*Mouse (16 species)*[+] *
*Ocelot**
*Orangutan*
*Oryx*
*Ostrich*[+]
*Otter*[+]
*Owl*[+] *
*Panda, giant*

7

*Panther, Florida**
*Parakeet+*
*Parrot+*
*Pheasant+*
*Possum+*
*Prairie dog+ **
*Pronghorn+ **
*Rat (8 species)+ **
*Rhinoceros+*
*Seal+*
*Squirrel, Carolina northern*
  *flying**
*Stork, oriental white*
*Tiger*
*Tortoise+ **
*Turtle+ **
*Vicuña*
*Wallaby+*
*Whale+*
*Wolf, gray**
*Wolf, red**
*Woodpecker+ **
*Zebra+ **

# 1

# Whooping Cranes

## Who's Stealing the Eggs?

It is a cool spring morning in May, and Ernie Kuyt is on a mission. He is in a helicopter flying low across the wet and grassy marshlands of northern Canada, searching the ground below. Suddenly he spots just what he's looking for. Ernie orders the pilot to drop down quickly. Then he jumps out of the chopper and into the wet marsh, so that he can grab his prey. What is he after? Whooping crane eggs!

The marsh is so wet, the water comes up to Ernie's thighs. But Ernie doesn't care. A little water won't stop him from reaching his goal. He heads straight for the nest a whooping crane built. It is a large pile of marsh grass, sitting just above water level.

There are two eggs in the nest, and they are a buff-olive color. Each one is about the size of a large orange. Ernie takes one egg and puts it in a heavy wool sock. Then he climbs back into the helicopter and hurries to another nest. There will probably be two eggs in that nest, too, and Ernie will again take one of them. Ernie is always careful to leave one egg in each nest.

Why is this man stealing whooping crane eggs? Doesn't he know that a *whooping crane* is one of the rarest birds in the world?

Actually, Ernie Kuyt knows all about whooping cranes. He is a biologist working for the Canadian Wildlife Service. He knows that whooping cranes usually lay two eggs, but raise only one chick. Most of the time, the other chick dies. So Ernie is trying to save whooping cranes from extinction by stealing and hatching their "extra" eggs.

## Meet the Whooping Crane

Imagine a beautiful big white bird that is 5 feet tall. Its head is bright red and its cheeks are red or black. Its legs are like thin black poles, and it has a long pointed beak. Its most striking feature is its long curving neck, which bends and arches when the bird looks around.

The whooping crane is graceful when standing, but it is even more lovely in flight. Its wings spread out to a full 7 feet across! Then you can see five black tips on each wing, fanning out like fingers.

But as soon as whooping cranes open their mouths, all the quiet beauty ends. The sound they make is a loud, harsh whooping call that gives the bird its name. And the whoop can be heard more than a mile away! Whooping cranes are loud because they have a very long windpipe to produce sound. The windpipe is coiled around inside their throats. If it were stretched out straight, the windpipe would be longer than the height of the bird.

While other birds are said to sing, whooping cranes are said to *bugle*. Sometimes they bugle to warn other cranes of danger. Sometimes they call to their young chicks. But the most interesting sounds are the calls

*When the whooping crane spreads its wings, the wings can stretch as much as 7 feet across.*

that a male and female pair make together. The male's call is different from the female's. His call is usually two long, low notes. The female's call is three higher-pitched notes. When they call in unison, it sounds like one bird bugling.

### Mates for Life

How can two cranes know each other well enough to sing duets together? How do they know when to start bugling, both at the same time? The answer probably has something to do with the fact that whooping cranes mate for life. Once a male and female have chosen each other and paired off, they spend all their time together. They choose a territory for their family and protect it together. They fly north together in summer and fly south in winter. They even dance together when they're in the right mood!

Dance? That's what scientists call the movements that cranes make when they're trying to attract their mate. And since the grown birds are probably taller than you are, it looks a lot like dancing! To dance, a whooping crane will flap its wings, bend its neck up and down, and strut around gracefully. If another crane responds by dancing too, it means the cranes like each other and will probably become mates.

Cranes are picky about selecting their mates. Scientists have observed young cranes trying to choose a mate and found that it is a lot like watching teenagers dating. Some cranes dance together a bit, then decide they just don't like each other. They seem to be saying they want a mate with a different personality. Once they find a good partner, however, cranes stay together until one of them dies.

### Summer Home, Winter Home

Strange as it may seem, all the whooping cranes in the wild now live in the same two places. One is a summer home, and the other a winter home. They spend their summers in Wood Buffalo National Park in Canada. The park is a completely deserted wetlands area—an ideal habitat for the cranes. The park has just what they need: marshy waters to catch frogs and fish, tall grasses and willows for nests, and plenty of other foods such as grains and insects.

One other trait makes the Canadian park perfect for

*Marshland makes the perfect home for the whooping crane. There are fish in the waters and tall grasses for nests.*

whoopers. It is very private. Because it is a wetlands, the area cannot be traveled by car or truck, so there are few people. The park is also somewhat isolated from the cranes' *predators,* animals that would hunt the cranes for food. Cranes can defend themselves against small animals, but large animals such as wolves, bears, and coyotes do sometimes find their way to whooping crane nests. For the most part, however, the cranes have the park to themselves.

In October of every year, the cranes leave Canada and begin to fly south. Covering up to 500 miles per day, they fly a total of about 2,500 miles, stopping to rest along the way. Sometimes they stop in one place for several days at a time. The cranes finally arrive about three weeks later in their winter home. The spot they choose is always the same. It is a wetlands area in southern Texas on the coastline of the Gulf of Mexico. This area is now called the Aransas National Wildlife Refuge.

Why do all the cranes go to Aransas? Well, it's like a family tradition. Each crane family stakes out its own territory and protects it from other cranes. Then, when the young cranes are old enough, after the first winter, the parents chase them away. These young cranes are called *subadults,* something like "teenager" cranes. But even though their parents have chased them away, the teenagers usually come back to the same spot where they spent their youth. They choose a territory of their own, very near their parents' winter home.

The winter habitat in Aransas is perfect for whooping cranes because it is a wetlands area, like the Canadian park up north, with plenty of food. Whoopers especially like the clams and crabs they find in the shallow southern waters. The cranes spend about half their day looking for food—and can eat as much as one clam per minute. That includes the time it takes them to dig the clams out of the sand!

Whooping cranes need wetlands to survive. But the wetlands all over America are disappearing as more and more wilderness areas are developed for people to use. Even in Aransas, the wetlands are getting smaller because the shoreline is being eroded by boats that travel through the nearby waterways. Each year about 2 acres of shoreline simply vanish, leaving a smaller habitat for the cranes. That's one reason why the whooping crane population is so small.

## Almost Extinct

There were never many whooping cranes in America. Even in the early 1800s, before the crane became endangered, there were only about 1,500 whoopers.

By 1941, however, there were only 22 whooping cranes left anywhere on the earth. The reason was the same problem that has threatened so many other animals—a shrinking habitat. Sixteen of the whoopers spent their summers together in Canada and migrated to Texas every winter. The other six birds lived year-round in Louisiana. By 1950, the Louisiana flock had died out completely. Whooping cranes were on their way to extinction.

Luckily, something had happened earlier that gave the whooping crane a fighting chance. In 1937, the U.S. government had decided to try to save the whooping crane. President Franklin D. Roosevelt had signed a law that made the southern coast of Texas into the Aransas National Wildlife Refuge, a protected spot for wildlife. That was the first step: protecting the cranes' habitat. Then in 1966, and again in 1973, Congress passed the Endangered Species Act. The act protected the whooping crane from hunters.

But one big question remained: Were there enough whooping cranes left for the species to survive? And if not, what could scientists do to help?

## Ernie's Stolen Eggs

Over the years, biologists in Canada have come up with several clever plans to help build up the flock of whooping cranes. But these days all the plans have one thing in common: They all begin with Ernie Kuyt, who goes out each spring to steal whooping crane eggs.

The first thing Ernie does is check each egg to make sure it has a live embryo in it. The test is simple: Ernie floats the egg in a bucket of warm water and watches carefully. If there is a live chick inside, the egg will rock or move. If the egg has a live embryo in it, Ernie puts it back into the nest and tests the other one. He wants to make sure that he leaves one good egg in each nest.

Once in a while, Ernie finds two bad eggs in a nest. In that case, he takes the bad eggs away and puts one good egg, collected from another crane's nest, in their place. With this sneaky system, Ernie is able to outsmart nature and make sure that every whooping crane has a chance to hatch a healthy chick.

After the eggs are collected, each one is put in a

heavy wool sock and taken back to the helicopter. There the eggs are put in a padded case. They are then carried by hand to their final destination, which is usually the Patuxent Wildlife Research Center in Laurel, Maryland. At this research center another crane, the sandhill crane, has been studied for years. And the whooping crane eggs are hatched by foster parents— *sandhill cranes.*

Most sandhill cranes are not endangered, so there are many more of them available than whooping cranes. Some have been raised and kept in captivity so that scientists can study them. Now these cranes help out with the whooping crane project. They sit on the whooper eggs and feed the whooper chicks when they first hatch. They also help teach the baby chicks to think of themselves as birds, and to be wary of human beings.

Captive sandhills make good parents for whoopers— up to a point. The problems arise when the time comes for the whooping cranes to leave home; that is, return to the wild. Then the whoopers don't seem to know what to do. Why not? Because their sandhill parents haven't taught them! Since the sandhill cranes were born in captivity, they have never *migrated,* or traveled from one place to another. For that reason, they don't know where to go. And since the sandhill cranes were fed by their keepers, they are not very good at hunting for food on their own. They can't teach the whooping cranes these basic skills.

And there's another disadvantage, too. Since the whooping cranes were raised by captive sandhills, the whoopers don't seem to know exactly what kind of bird they are! That causes a real problem when it's time for the whoopers to mate. They can't choose a mate from among wild whooping cranes.

Most important of all, captive birds don't know how to protect themselves from predators in the wild. Releasing a captive-born bird into the wild is a little like letting a 4-year-old child loose in the middle of a big city. The child would feel totally confused, and could get hurt pretty quickly.

Unfortunately, that's what has happened to captive-born whooping cranes when they've been released into the wild. They don't know about migration. They don't know how to select and defend a territory. They don't even know how to go about choosing a mate. In fact, none of the whooping cranes raised in captivity have ever managed to mate with another crane, either in the wild or in captivity. Maybe they have spent too much time with sandhill cranes, so they don't realize that they are whoopers.

Still, scientists are optimistic about the whooping crane project, especially the egg switching. Just look at the results! Before the egg switching began, the whoopers were coming back—but *very* slowly. From a total of 16 birds in 1941, the Canadian flock increased on its own to more than 40 birds by 1967. Then in 1967, Ernie Kuyt started stealing and switching eggs. Since then the wild flock of 40 whoopers in Canada has more than tripled! By 1992 there were about 150 whoopers in the wild. That's a major success story in the world of endangered species.

# 2

# Tigers
## Big Killer Cats

The year was 1932. The place was the small village of Kanda near the Himalaya Mountains in India. A man-eating *Bengal tiger* was on the loose, and the villagers feared for their lives. So far, the man-eater had killed and eaten seven people in three months. No one dared move about the countryside for fear that the tiger would strike again.

Because the villagers were afraid to go into the forest to find grass for their cattle, the animals were dying. And the people didn't dare guard their wheat fields, so the deer that roamed at night were free to eat all of the crops.

There was only one thing to do—send for the one man who could track down the tiger and kill it. That man was Jim Corbett, an Englishman who had been born in India and lived there nearly all his life. Fearless from a very young age, Corbett shot his first leopard when he was 9 years old. Even when he was too young to have a gun, he hunted game animals in the forests of India using a bow and arrow or a *catapult,* a device for hurling rocks or other objects. Corbett was so interested in wildlife that he learned how to make the calls of many wild animals. And he was brave enough to call to them in the dark of night! His calls sounded so real that many animals answered.

As he grew older, Corbett became an expert big-game hunter—and tigers were his specialty. Corbett knew how to track the dangerous tiger through the deep brush of its own territory. He knew how to wait patiently for hours or even days, sitting in a tree near a spot where a tiger might come. He knew how to read tiger tracks. He could recognize a specific tiger, just from the distinctive paw prints it made on the ground!

Over the years, Corbett tracked and shot dozens of tigers—probably more than any other big-game hunter in the world. And whenever there was a man-eating tiger on the loose—one that had developed a habit of killing human beings—Corbett was the person who was asked to destroy it.

But in 1932, when the villagers of Kanda sent for Corbett, he was a bit reluctant to come. After years of hunting, he had begun to feel sickened by the act of killing animals. The turning point had come about a year earlier, when Corbett had watched three hunters shoot 300 ducks in one day—many more ducks than they could possibly eat. Corbett decided then and there that he would never again shoot just for the sport of it.

Killing a man-eating tiger, however, was not sport. It was a job, a lifesaving job, and few other people were qualified to do it. Corbett agreed to stalk the tiger. But he didn't do it for money. The villagers were poor and could not pay. Corbett did it because he believed that once a tiger had gotten into the habit of eating human beings, it would never stop hunting humans.

It took some time for Corbett to find the tiger's territory. When he did, he was able to kill the man-eater with two quick shots.

After this job, Jim Corbett became more and more concerned about preserving wildlife. Instead of shooting animals with a gun, he began to "shoot" them with his camera. He took many beautiful photographs of the animals that he loved so much.

He also worried that tiger habitats were being destroyed. In India, forests were rapidly being cut down as more and more towns were being built. Corbett was afraid that the tiger would become extinct if something wasn't done soon to help save the endangered animal.

## Meet the Tiger

Tigers are the biggest of the big cats. At 600 pounds and more than 12 feet long, the *Siberian tiger,* which is the largest of all tigers, is even bigger than a lion. An average Bengal tiger is a little smaller. It weighs about 420 pounds and measures 10 feet long.

There are eight species of tigers, but they are all very much alike. They behave similarly, spending their time raising cubs and stalking prey for food. The greatest differences among tigers are their size and color. Some tigers have thick black stripes. Others have thin stripes. Some have a yellow-brown background color. Others wear their black stripes on a background of dark red.

Tigers have lived in many parts of the world, including Turkey, Iran, China, Korea, Russia, and the islands of Java and Bali in Indonesia. But most of the tigers remaining in the wild are Bengal tigers, native to India.

Bengal tigers, like all tigers, need three things for survival. They need a thickly forested habitat, so that they can hide while stalking their prey. They need water. And they need a good supply of prey animals. Tigers must eat about 15 pounds of meat each day.

## Feast or Famine

Although a tiger eats more than 5,000 pounds of food per year, it doesn't eat three regular meals a day. In fact, some days it eats almost nothing—not even small snacks such as turtles, fish, or birds. Other days, when a tiger kills a large animal, the tiger will have a feast.

What does a tiger think is a tasty meal? A nice big water buffalo is always a good choice, as far as tigers are concerned. Deer, antelope, and cattle are also favorite foods, especially since they are big enough to last for more than one meal. Sometimes a tiger will attack a small rhinoceros or a young elephant. When tigers kill a large animal, they drag the kill off to a private spot so that they don't have to share their food.

A tiger can eat up to 50 pounds of meat at one sitting. Then the tiger covers the carcass to hide it, and takes a catnap. Later that day, the tiger will eat again and again. A deer carcass may last for two days, and the tiger eats everything except the bones and the contents of the deer's stomach.

Tigers are strong and fast, but they can't chase their prey for long distances. Instead, tigers stalk their victims, usually sneaking up on them at night. Even in the daytime, though, the tiger's black stripes and orange coloring blend in with the jungle, helping to *cam-*

*This Bengal tiger is ready to pounce on its next meal. Tigers can run fast for only a short time, so they sneak up on their prey and then spring on it quickly.*

ouflage the tiger. This means the coloring and markings allow the tiger to blend into its surroundings, so that it can stalk grazing animals without being seen.

## Baby Tigers

Tigers are solitary animals, which means that they prefer to keep to themselves. Males and females get together only during mating season. After that, the male goes off again to defend his territory, and the female waits to give birth.

When the cubs are born, they weigh only 3 or 4 pounds. There are usually two or three cubs in a litter, although there can be as many as nine. Until they are about 2 months old, the cubs stay safely in a *den,* a place where animals live. The den can be anywhere— in a cave, a rock shelter, or even a spot in thick bushes. A mother tiger nurses her young in the den, just as a pet cat nurses her kittens.

When the cubs are old enough, they leave the den with their mother to go out into the world. They begin to prowl around with their mother, who teaches them how to hunt for food. It takes two years before the young tigers can survive on their own.

Most tigers live about 20 years. Adult tigers have few predators. Sometimes a tiger dies when it is hunted by a pack of wild dogs or gored by a water buffalo. But usually the tiger has no enemies other than humans. There is one exception, though. Occa-

*Mother tigers carry their cubs by the neck, just like house cats.*

sionally, an *albino,* or white, tiger is born. These albino babies don't live very long because of their coloring. Albino tigers have black stripes, just like other tigers, but the background color of their fur is white. With blue eyes and soft white fur, they are quite beautiful. But unfortunately, their light coloring is a dead giveaway in the jungle. They are so easy to spot that they are usually killed by other predators such as wild oxen, wild boars, or crocodiles.

## Man-eaters! Why?

As long as there is enough food in the wild, most tigers do not become man-eaters. Even when the tiger's wooded habitat is destroyed, tigers don't choose to eat people first. Instead, they turn to cattle. Given a choice, most tigers prefer to stay far away from human beings.

But every so often a tiger turns into what some people call a man-eater. It seems to happen most often in an area in northern India called the Sundarbans Delta. Here, more than 100 people were once killed by tigers over a 3-year period. Scientists are trying to figure out why the tigers in that area are more likely to kill human beings.

One theory is that people are living too close to the tigers' habitat. Some scientists say that people and tigers just don't mix. They should be kept far away from each other.

Jim Corbett had his own ideas about man-eaters. He said that ordinary tigers would only attack people under three circumstances: (1) if the tiger was wounded by a hunter, (2) if it was a mother protecting her cubs, or (3) if it was disturbed while eating its prey. But according to Corbett, once a tiger learns to kill human beings, it never forgets. Once a man-eater, always a man-eater, Corbett believed.

## Corbett National Park

Although Jim Corbett realized that it was sometimes necessary to kill a man-eating tiger, he spent the last 20 years of his life (from the mid-1930s to 1955) trying to preserve tigers. And he was alarmed when he noticed that the number of tigers was dwindling. In fact, there had been about 50,000 tigers in India in the late 1800s, when Corbett was born. By 1972, the number sank to an all-time low of 2,000.

In 1936, when big-game hunting was at the height of its popularity, Corbett began to speak out publicly against shooting animals for sport. His views were extremely unpopular at the time, but he didn't care. He believed that a wildlife preserve should be set aside so that tigers and other wild animals could be kept safe from hunters—and he said so every chance he got. Within a year, 100 square miles of land in northern India were set aside as a wildlife sanctuary. At the same time, Corbett started a magazine called *Indian Wildlife*.

Corbett's ideas finally began to be accepted. After his death, the wildlife sanctuary was expanded and was named Corbett National Park. And in 1973, India began a program to create more tiger preserves to help save the tiger from extinction.

Today many species of tigers in other parts of the world are endangered. Scientists think the *Bali tiger* in Indonesia is already extinct. And there are so few *Javan tigers* remaining that their future is doubtful. With only a few hundred Siberian tigers remaining in the wild—in the far eastern parts of Russia, northern North Korea, and northern China—these animals, too, may not have a chance for survival.

However, the number of Bengal tigers is increasing. There are now more than 5,000 of them throughout India. Interestingly enough, they owe their comeback in large part to the man who had started out as a big-game hunter—Jim Corbett—but ended up as one of the tiger's best friends.

# 3

## Sea Turtles
### On Turtle Patrol

Shhh! No talking allowed!

It is a warm summer night on Pritchard Island, off the coast of Georgia, and the *loggerhead sea turtles* are coming. Or at least everyone on the beach hopes so. The people are all waiting quietly in the dark for the female turtles to come out of the water and lay their eggs in the sand. When the eggs are laid, the people will dig them up and move them.

What's going on? This is turtle patrol!

Turtle patrol is a nickname for a project to save the loggerheads. Every year in June, the turtle conservation project takes place on several beaches along the Atlantic coast, including this beach in Georgia. Here scientists sleep during the day, so that they can stay up late every night. They walk the beaches in the dark, waiting for the female loggerheads to arrive and lay their eggs.

### Meet the Loggerhead

The loggerhead turtle is a huge reptile with a reddish-brown shell. Like most sea turtles, it almost never leaves the water—except to lay eggs. But that doesn't mean the turtle stays underwater all the time.

Most loggerheads come up to the surface to breathe about once every two minutes. And some can hold their breath for even longer—20 minutes or more!

When a female loggerhead does leave the water and come up onto the beach to lay eggs, it's a struggle. An average loggerhead weighs 300 pounds and is about 4 feet long. Its front legs look like flippers and are more suited to swimming than crawling. So it's hard work for the turtle to drag itself across the sand.

Once the female loggerheads are on the beach, they become very busy. They dig a hole about as big as they are. They use all four legs to kick and scoop sand to make the nest. Then they deposit their eggs. Sometimes a female lays as many as 200 eggs at a time! Each egg is the size of a Ping-Pong ball. Before she leaves, the mother covers the eggs with sand to keep them safe.

Unfortunately, the eggs *aren't* safe. Raccoons prowl around the beach at night. So do dogs and cats. These animals like to eat the eggs. And the dogs might even attack the female turtle. That's why she hurries back to the water as fast as she can.

Loggerhead turtles are only one kind of sea turtle. Some other species are the Pacific green turtle, the hawksbill, the Ridley, and the giant leatherback. These turtles are found throughout the world's oceans, and all of these sea turtles have a lot in common. They all lay eggs in nests on the beach. And they all are threatened or endangered.

Loggerhead turtle eggs must stay in the nest for about 60 days. Most of the eggs are usually eaten by predators before they hatch. Raccoons, foxes, coyotes,

*Loggerhead turtles like this one swimming off the coast of Florida weigh about 300 pounds. They almost never leave the water, except when the females lay eggs.*

dogs, cats, and even people have been known to dig up and eat sea turtle eggs. And after the eggs hatch, many young turtles are eaten by rats, snakes, and large sea birds. Out of every 100 eggs, fewer than 10 baby turtles are likely to survive and to make a successful trek from the beach to the sea.

### Life at Sea

If the baby turtles reach the water—and if they aren't eaten right away by big fish—they soon begin to grow. Baby loggerheads grow quickly at first because they eat whatever is around. Their diet includes little crabs, jellyfish, squid, tiny fish, and plants such as seaweed. Surprisingly, though, loggerheads do not become breeding adults for many years. Their rate of growth varies widely, depending in part on the food supply.

Once they are full-grown, loggerheads and other sea turtles have only three enemies in the water: sharks, killer whales, and human beings. In the past, people caught sea turtles and ate them. Now that the turtles are endangered, it is against the law to hunt them in the United States and in other countries.

But shrimp fishers still accidentally catch turtles when they become trapped in shrimping nets. Sometimes the *shrimpers,* as people who fish for shrimp are called, can remove the turtles from the nets and let them go. But sometimes the turtles die.

To keep sea turtles out of shrimp nets, most shrimpers are now required to use a TED. That stands for Turtle Excluder Device, a special kind of net that allows trapped turtles to escape. But some shrimpers don't want to use the TED. They argue that the device lets some shrimp escape, too.

The other big problem for sea turtles is the same one that many endangered animals face: loss of habitat. For turtles, the problem isn't that they're losing the sea. Instead they are losing the *beaches* where they lay their eggs.

In many places, beaches are getting smaller and more crowded. People have built houses and hotels there. When there are more people, there are also more pet dogs. And dogs eat turtle eggs. Lights from houses shine on the beach at night, scaring the female turtles away.

That's why scientists are going on turtle patrol. They are trying to give the endangered loggerheads a helping hand and a better chance to survive.

## Like Mother, Like Child

Loggerheads may be getting help from scientists, but something female loggerheads *don't* need help with is determining the right time to lay their eggs. They know just when to do it. For one thing, they always lay eggs at night. In the dark they have some protection from predators.

Loggerheads also usually lay their eggs at high tide. And even if it's not high tide, they know to lay their eggs above the high-tide line! To understand why this is so intelligent, you have to know a little about the water and the shore.

High tide occurs when the water comes in toward shore, higher up on the beach. Low tide is the opposite. It occurs when the water has gone back out toward the sea, leaving more beach exposed.

If the turtle eggs were laid near the water's edge during low tide—and then the tide came in—the turtle eggs would never hatch. Why? Because sea turtles need to breathe. Before they hatch, which takes 2 months, turtle embryos get air through the eggshell. But if the eggs were underwater, no air could pass through the shell. Female loggerheads outsmart the tides by laying their eggs where they will never be underwater.

Here's another interesting fact about loggerheads.

When the females lay their eggs, they always return to the same beach where they themselves hatched! Loggerheads may swim around in the ocean all year, traveling hundreds of miles. But when it's time to lay eggs, they always find their way home.

Newly hatched turtles, called *hatchlings,* are smart, too. They have to be. Their mothers aren't around to teach them what to do! But even without being taught, the babies seem to know that the beach isn't a very safe place. They don't hang around there very long. As soon as they hatch, they run down to the water as fast as their legs can carry them. One turtle expert called hatchlings "tiny nonstop windup toys." They go so fast, it takes only a few minutes for them to make the trip to the sea.

And guess what? These little hatchlings seem to know about the tides—just like their mothers. If the tide is low when they hatch, it is a longer distance from the nest to the water. So the hatchlings stay in the nest and wait for high tide. During high tide, the baby turtles don't have to travel so far to get to the water.

## Turtle Patrol

Scientists on Pritchard Island have been going on turtle patrol since 1981. The patrol takes place during June and July, when loggerheads are laying eggs on beaches along the Atlantic coast. As soon as scientists see a female leaving a nest, they dig the eggs up and put them in a burlap bag. Then they carry the eggs to a newly dug nest in the sand, just 100 yards away. These nests are inside a fenced-in protected area. The fence keeps raccoons and other predators out, so that more eggs will survive and hatch.

Two months later, these "captive" eggs hatch, also at night. And amazingly enough, they usually hatch during high tide. The scientists, along with some volunteer teenagers and adults, stand by at this time as well. They make sure the fence doesn't get in the way as the hatchlings scramble down to the sea.

On Pritchard Island the beach is only about 2 miles long. Still, in this one small area there can be several hundred nests each year! That's a lot of eggs to dig up and replant.

If you would like to go on a turtle patrol, you might be able to join a sea turtle watch trip when you are a teenager. An environmental group called Wilderness Southeast sponsors these trips. Teenagers must be at least 14 years old, and must be accompanied by an adult. For more information, contact the group at this address:

Wilderness Southeast
711 Sandtown Road
Savannah, GA 31410
Phone: (912) 897-5108

# 4

# Komodo Dragons
## Island Monsters!

Imagine that you are an explorer, searching the islands of Indonesia between Borneo and Australia. The islands are far from the mainland, and almost no one lives there, so you don't know what to expect. You are walking through the jungle when suddenly something moves in the bushes nearby—something very large.

Then you get your first look at what's ahead—a dragon-like creature that's 10 feet long and weighs about 300 pounds. Its whole body is flattened and low to the ground, and every inch of it, including the huge powerful legs and long tail, is covered with grayish-brown scales. Sharp claws stick out from the ends of the creature's feet, and when it opens its mouth, you can see jagged teeth. As if that isn't enough of a sight, you notice that this dragon-like monster is flicking its forked tongue at you!

That is probably exactly what happened when European explorers first discovered the *Komodo dragon* in 1912. It was the world's largest living lizard, and it existed only on four small islands in Indonesia. One was the island of Komodo, which gives the animal its name. The other three were the neighboring islands of Rintja, Flores, and Padar.

What did the early explorers do when they came upon this startling beast? Good question! They might have climbed a tree, but that wouldn't have helped. Komodo dragons are tree climbers, too. Jumping into the ocean probably wouldn't have worked either. These giant lizards are great swimmers and could have followed the human intruders into the water. As a last resort, the explorers might have tried to run. But if the Komodo dragon was close enough, it would have caught the adventurers before they got very far. Komodo dragons can move very quickly. They are able to run up to 11 miles per hour, though only for short periods of time.

### Meet the Komodo Dragon

Komodo dragons—also called *monitors*—are members of the reptile family. That means they are related to other animals that crawl on their bellies or walk on short legs, breathe the air, have a backbone, and usually have scales or bony plates. In other words, they are related to snakes, lizards, and turtles—even sea turtles.

Unlike sea turtles, Komodo dragons do not spend most of their time in the water. Since they are meat-eaters, they live on land, looking for food. Komodo dragons aren't picky about what they eat. They'll hunt birds, rats, pigs, chickens, monkeys, deer, and even smaller Komodo dragons. An average adult can eat 5 pounds of meat per minute. Often they simply swallow small animals whole. They even devour the horns, hooves, and bones of their prey.

Komodo dragons can smell their prey from quite a

distance away. For that reason, it's easy to get these lizards to come close to you. All you have to do is put out a dead animal and let it begin to rot! That's what officials do in Indonesia when they want to attract a Komodo dragon for tourists to see. Before long the hungry lizard shows up and starts to feast.

The only thing Komodo dragons won't eat is an early breakfast. That's because, like all lizards, they are *cold-blooded*, which means their body temperature drops and rises according to the temperature of the surroundings. When the air temperature cools at night, so does the lizard's temperature. The Komodo dragon's body temperature is still cool when it wakes up in the morning. It isn't really ready for food or any other activity. It needs to warm up in the sun first, before it has the energy to hunt, kill, or eat.

*Komodo dragons in Indonesia eat a goat carcass for lunch. Komodos can eat a lot—up to 5 pounds of food per minute!*

## Terrible Teeth

If a Komodo dragon sneaks up on you, you're in big trouble. Why? Because fully grown Komodo dragons are big enough and powerful enough to grab their prey, even human beings, in an instant.

The worst part of the Komodo dragon's bite is its terrible teeth. Like some sharks, these lizards can easily tear the meat off their prey because their teeth are jagged, or *saw-toothed.* Sometimes Komodo dragons eat food that is already rotten. They may feed on *carrion,* animals that are already dead or that have been killed by some other animal.

## Baby Dragons

Like nearly all lizards, the female Komodo dragon lays eggs. She deposits them in a deep burrow that she digs. The eggs are leathery, and there may be a dozen in each burrow. As soon as the eggs are laid, the mother leaves. She doesn't stay around to raise her young because Komodo dragons don't live in families. When the babies hatch, they are on their own. They must find their own food and take care of themselves.

In their first year of life, young Komodo dragons often hide in trees, eating insects. They stay in trees to avoid being eaten by other animals. Their gray-brown scales provide camouflage because they match the color of the tree bark. Still, many of the young are killed by birds or snakes or larger Komodo dragons.

Newly hatched Komodo dragons are about 1 foot long. Each year the young dragons grow another foot in length. Within five or six years, they are about 6 feet long—big enough to protect themselves from almost anything.

## Pet Dinosaurs?

With its prehistoric-looking scaly skin and jagged teeth, the Komodo dragon looks a lot like a small dinosaur. In other words, pretty scary! And to the scientists who first gave the animal its name, it looked like a monster or a dragon. So who would want to keep this creature as a pet?

The answer is, lots of people. In recent years, many people who keep exotic animals as pets have wanted to add a Komodo dragon to their collection. With Komodo dragons being captured by collectors, there are fewer of them living on their island homes. As a result, they have become endangered. Komodo dragon adults have no natural enemies aside from human beings.

Another reason the dragons are endangered is that their chief food source is disappearing. The island people hunt deer and wild goats for food, so there are fewer large animals for the dragons to eat.

Now that Komodo dragons are on the Endangered Species List, it is illegal to capture them and sell them without permission. So forget about having your very own "pet dinosaur." But if you'd like to get a better look at a Komodo dragon—at a safe distance—you might want to visit the National Zoo in Washington, D.C., or the San Diego Zoo in California.

# 5

## Rhinoceroses
### Outsmarting the Horn Hunters

A helicopter roars over the open grasslands of Zimbabwe, in southern Africa. Below, there is a herd of *white rhinoceroses,* one of the rarest large animals on Earth. A man leans out of the helicopter with a rifle in his hands. He fires a shot. It hardly makes a sound, but almost immediately a rhinoceros falls to the ground.

Within a few minutes, the helicopter lands and the man jumps out. Carrying a chainsaw, he runs toward the animal. Then the whir of the saw pierces the peaceful quiet of the African plains as the man begins to cut off the rhino's horn!

What is happening? Is it incidents such as this that have made the rhinoceros endangered?

No, just the opposite. This is one method that park rangers in Africa are using to try to save the rhino from extinction. The park rangers shoot the rhino with a *tranquilizer dart gun*—not bullets. The gun shoots a drug into the animal to put it to sleep safely and temporarily. Then, while the animal is quiet, the rangers saw off the rhino's horn.

Rhinoceros horn is very valuable. Many animals are illegally killed each year for their horns. To prevent this slaughter, experts are trying to make the animals less attractive. The idea is simple: If a rhino doesn't have a horn, maybe no one will want to shoot it.

## Meet the Big Bullies

Imagine a pickup truck lumbering 35 miles an hour in your direction. On the front of the truck there is a hard, pointed weapon that is almost indestructible. The truck weighs about 8,000 pounds and is 6 feet high and about 16 feet long. And the truck driver is in a bad mood! Well, that's what it's like to be attacked by a rhinoceros. Luckily, though, rhinos don't attack people very often.

The rhinoceros is a vegetarian. And since rhinos

*This 3-day-old rhino may be small now, but it will grow up to weigh as much as 8,000 pounds!*

don't eat meat, they usually don't attack other animals. Most of the time, a rhino uses its horns to attack or *charge* other rhinos!

Male rhinos, called *bulls,* do most of the charging. They are very *territorial,* which means they want their own area or territory for themselves. And they want other bulls to keep out. The territory a rhino chooses is called his *home range.*

Sometimes a bull will actually attack other males who come into his home range. But often the charge is just a "bluff," meant as a warning to the other rhinos. It tells them that the bull is willing to fight to stay in control of his territory.

The strangest thing a rhino does is bluff charging when nothing is there. All of a sudden a bull starts running and charging—at nothing! It looks weird, but scientists think there's an easy explanation. Rhinos have very poor eyesight. When a rhino bull makes such an unnecessary charge, it may just be that he *thinks* there's another rhino nearby. The excited animal can't see well enough to know for sure!

### One Horn or Two?

Rhinoceroses come in different sizes and colors. They also have either square lips or hooked lips, and one horn or two. It all depends on their species. There are five species in all.

First, take a look at the *black rhino* of southern Africa. It lives in South Africa, Namibia, Zimbabwe, and southern Mozambique. Weighing between 2,000 and 4,000 pounds, it is about medium-sized for a rhino. It has two horns. The longer horn is in front and can measure up to 52 inches. The shorter horn is right behind it.

Black rhinos are *solitary*. They like to be by themselves most of the time. And they prefer to stay in the jungle, rather than out in the open African plains. It's probably just as well that black rhinos are loners, because they are known for having bad tempers. They charge more often than any other rhino species.

So how do you keep a black rhino happy? Leave it alone with plenty to eat. Its favorite foods are juicy twigs from trees and fresh young shoots from bushes. Black rhinos are picky about what they eat, which is why their hooked lips come in handy. They can use their hooked top lip to feel around for food and grab it. Then they chomp down with their teeth.

*White rhinos,* on the other hand, are more easygoing than black rhinos. And it's a good thing, too, since white rhinos are almost twice as big! They weigh between 5,000 and 8,000 pounds. These truck-sized animals are friendly with each other. They live in small family groups of three, four, or five. The bulls will charge one another to defend their home-range territory, but they don't fight as much as black rhinos do.

White rhinos live in northern and southern Africa. They like open grassy areas, as long as there are bushes nearby for shade. They aren't as picky about their food as black rhinos are. White rhinos have square lips, and use them to graze on dry grass the same way cattle do. Like black rhinos, they have two horns, one in front of the other.

But if you think white rhinos are big, you'll be even more impressed with the *Indian rhino*. It is the biggest

*The white rhino uses its square lips to feed on the short grass.*

of all, weighing up to 8,800 pounds. These animals can be 6½ feet tall at the shoulder! Luckily, they also are not as ill-tempered as black rhinos, and they have only one horn. Like all rhinos, they are strictly vegetarian.

The smallest species of rhino lives on the islands of Java and Sumatra, in the Indian Ocean south of the Asian continent. They tend to live in mountain forests and thick jungles, as long as there is water nearby.

The *Sumatran rhino* is small, weighing an average of 1,500 pounds, and both males and females have two horns. The *Javan rhino* weighs as much as 1 ton— 2,000 pounds. The males have one horn, but some of the females, or *cows,* have no horn at all.

## A Day in the Wallow

To cool themselves off, all rhinos like to spend time in pools of muddy water, called *wallows.* Rhinos drink the water from the wallow, and then roll around in the mud. The mud coats their skin with a wet layer that keeps them cool. Rhinos don't have sweat glands so they can't perspire. Wallowing in the mud cools them down and also keeps insects from biting their skin.

## Who Wants the Horn?

In the 1970s, black rhinos were not endangered. There were about 60,000 of them in Africa. But by 1992, only about 3,000 remained.

The northern white rhino has also become endangered, although its numbers have always been smaller than those of the black rhino. In the 1970s there were about 2,000 northern white rhinos. Today there are only a few dozen alive.

45

Javan, Sumatran, and Indian rhinos are nearly extinct as well. Why are these species endangered? Most have been hunted and killed for their horns.

Rhinoceros horn is valuable for two reasons. It is made of *keratin,* a substance that is similar to the protein found in human fingernails. Strong, but easy to cut, keratin makes a good material to carve. In Yemen, a country in the Middle East, rhino horns are carved into expensive handles for daggers. These daggers are status symbols in Yemen, and can cost $15,000 each!

But dagger handles aren't the only use for rhino horn. In Asia, many people believe that powdered rhino horn is a good medicine. They use it to cure fevers. Because so many people want this medicine, the price of rhino horn goes up and up. In some places, rhino horn is worth $450 a pound! That means that one horn could bring in as much as $20,000.

Even though it is now illegal to hunt rhinos—and illegal to buy or sell rhino horn in many countries—*poachers* continue the hunt. A poacher is a person who hunts and kills animals illegally. These lawbreakers are willing to risk getting caught, because there is so much money to be made from the sale of rhino horns.

That's why the governments of Namibia and Zimbabwe, in southern Africa, decided to try a daring idea. In 1989, Namibia began dehorning the rhinos—before the poachers could do it. In 1991, Zimbabwe joined in. Using dart guns to put the rhinos to sleep, animal experts were able to cut off the horns of 59 animals living in Zimbabwe's Hwange National Park. They hoped that when poachers saw the rhinos had no horns, the thieves would go away.

*White rhinos like this mother and baby are endangered because some people kill rhinos for their horns. Rhino horns have sold for more than $20,000.*

At first, the plan didn't work. Some poachers killed a few rhinos anyway. But experts think it was because the poachers couldn't see that the rhino horns had been removed. After a few months, poachers began to leave the dehorned animals alone.

Now other African countries are considering dehorning their rhinos. And for people who hate to see an animal's natural defenses removed, it's nice to know that these rhinos will not have to be hornless forever.

Why not? Because if a rhino's horn is cut or broken, it grows back. Then the rhino can once again use its horns to defend its territory. Of course, when the horns grow back, the poachers are likely to return as well.

47

# 6

## California Condors

### Zoos to the Rescue

On Easter Sunday in 1987, Pete Bloom crouched in a forest in Los Angeles County, California, beside the carcass of a dead goat. Above him soared a huge bird with a wingspan of more than 9 feet. The shadow it cast was enormous. The bird was so large that someone else might have mistaken it for a small airplane.

But Bloom knew what it was. It was the very last *California condor* still living in the wild. All the others had been captured already.

Soon the condor landed near the dead goat and began to eat it. That's exactly what Pete hoped the bird would do. He had put the meat there as bait. Quickly he fired a shot. BOOM! A giant net sprang out of his cannon, trapping the condor.

### An Important Decision

The day the last California condor was captured was a sad day for scientists. Biologists like Pete Bloom and others had been trying to save the condor from extinction. They hoped the condor would always be able to fly wild and free.

It was also a sad day for the Chumash Indians of southern California. To them, the condor was an im-

48

portant part of their religion. They believed a condor carried a person's spirit to the afterlife.

But little by little, condors had been dying out. Two hundred years ago, there were 2,000 of them in California. But by 1983 there were only 21 birds left in the wild.

Scientists realized that they had to make an important decision: either leave a handful of birds alone and hope for the best, or capture the birds and try to breed them in captivity.

Many people argued fiercely about the problem. Some said that if the condors were captured, they would never be wild again. Others said that if the condors were left in the wild, they would become extinct. Then there would be no chance to ever see a living California condor again.

Before scientists could decide what to do, they had to think about what the condor needed. What kind of habitat did the condor have to have in order to survive?

## Meet the California Condor

The California condor is a bird of prey, the second largest bird in the world. The only bird larger is its cousin, the *Andean condor* of South America, with a wingspan of 10 feet. The Andean condor is also endangered.

Picture a bird 4 feet tall, standing in your bedroom. When it spread its wings, the tips could touch two opposite walls. A single feather from a California condor can be as long as your mother's or father's arm!

In the air, condors are beautiful. They soar on warm

*With a wingspan of 9 feet, the California condor is the second largest bird in the world. It can fly very fast—up to 50 miles per hour.*

air currents, sometimes flying 50 miles an hour. They can easily cover 150 miles in a day.

But up close—watch out! They have big curved beaks that are used for ripping and tearing prey. Their fearsome-looking bald heads are red. The only "decoration" is a little ruff around an otherwise naked neck. And then there are the claws!

Like other vultures, condors eat carrion, animals that have died or been killed by something else. Many years ago, there was carrion all along the California coast. Seals, whales, and other fish that died were washed up on shore. Today, however, there are fewer whales and seals left in the ocean. In fact, they are now endangered, too.

In recent years, California condors have eaten deer, cattle, and sheep. Often, the deer have been shot by hunters. When the condors eat the deer, they also eat the lead bullets. This causes lead poisoning, and the birds die.

Dead cattle and sheep are a good source of food for condors. But they can be a good source of trouble, too. Some farmers claim that the condors kill their sheep or calves. These farmers sometimes shoot at the birds to protect their livestock.

Other farmers put out poisoned animals as bait to kill predatory animals. But if the condor eats the bait, the poison kills the condor—just as it would have killed the coyote or fox it was intended for. All in all, it hasn't been easy being a condor!

When it's time to mate, condors are very loyal. They mate for life, selecting one partner and spending the next 35 years together. They nest in caves in sandstone mountains, high above sea level. There, the females lay only one egg every 2 years.

When a baby condor hatches, the parents feed it bits of meat until the hatchling is old enough to fly. It takes several months for the baby condor to fly. Young condors don't go off on their own until they are 2 years old.

### Caged or Free?

If you were one of the condor experts, what would you have done in the 1980s? Would you have captured all the wild condors and tried to breed them in zoos? Or would you have hoped that the 21 condors remaining in 1983 could exist on their own in the wild?

*This baby condor stays close to its nest, a cave high in the mountains. Young condors don't go off on their own until they are 2 years old.*

To help them decide, the experts first looked at the California condor. Then they looked at California.

They saw beaches, surfers, and Disneyland. They saw freeways, Hollywood, and movie stars. They saw millions of cars, and crowds of people. But they did not see much wilderness area where giant vultures could nest undisturbed. And they did not see a food supply of carrion that was safe for the condors to eat.

People had moved into the condors' neighborhood. Now there was only a small wild area, just north of Los Angeles, that was suitable condor habitat.

For a while, the scientists tried two approaches. They captured some of the condors, and left some in the wild. But by 1984, there were only 16 condors remaining in the wild. And then 7 of those birds died.

That's when the U.S. Fish and Wildlife Service decided that scientists must capture the rest of the condors—before they, too, were lost forever.

## Condor Eggs and Puppet Shows

Even before the last wild birds were captured, the number of California condors increased. Why? Because scientists came up with a clever plan. In 1983, they removed an egg from a wild condor's nest in southern California. When the female condor saw that the egg was gone, she laid another one. In the meantime, the first egg was taken to the Los Angeles Zoo and hatched in captivity.

The same trick was used with all the captive condors. Pretty soon, condor parents were producing two or three chicks a year, instead of just one. Some of the chicks were hatched at the Los Angeles Zoo. Others were hatched at the San Diego Zoo.

There was only one problem. Who was going to feed all these baby condors? Believe it or not, the answer was condor puppets!

Zoo experts knew that if human beings fed the baby condors, the birds would become tame. They would not acquire the survival skills they would need when they were released in the wild one day.

So all baby condors raised at the zoos are fed by puppets. A person puts the condor puppet on his or her hand, and uses the puppet's beak to hold the food.

Zookeepers make sure that the condors don't see peo-

*A condor puppet is used to feed a condor chick. If a baby condor sees human beings feeding it, it will become tame and lose its survival skills.*

ple or hear their voices much. That's one of the reasons the condors are in a private section of the zoo. They are not on exhibit where visitors can see them.

## Return of the Condors

By October 1991 there were more than 50 condors living in two California zoos. The captive-breeding program was going well. And enough chicks had been born for scientists to conclude it was time to let some condors fly wild and free again.

That month, two captive-born condors were taken to a *roost* in a forest north of Los Angeles. A roost is a place where birds perch or settle. A condor roost usually is a cave or protected ledge up high, where condors can make a nest. At first, the condor roost was enclosed in a mesh net, to keep the condors from flying away. A few months later, in January 1992, when the condors were used to their new surroundings, the birds were set free.

How did they like their new life-style? They liked it just fine. They flew along the same paths that condors had always used. They roosted on the same ledges. They seemed to know how to behave as condors always had!

The only difference was that scientists did not want the condors to find their own food. Eating poisoned carrion was one of the reasons condors were dying out in the first place.

So biologists put clean meat out for the condors. No one knows whether these captive-born condors could survive on their own if they weren't being fed by the scientists. But the experts don't want to find out—not for a while, anyway. They think it is better to feed the condors right now than risk letting them find their own, unhealthy food.

At the end of the year, in December, six more condors were released in the same area.

On that release day, everyone celebrated. The Chumash Indians were there. They blessed the land and opened the mesh netting to let the condors fly free. Everyone was happy to see the California condor return to the air.

But has the condor been saved from extinction? It's too early to know. Still, now that condors are being bred in captivity, they have a fighting chance. They have been brought back from the brink of extinction—and are once again soaring over their native California home.

# 7

# Saving the Animals

Most people agree that the number one enemy of endangered animals is human beings. But guess what? People can also be endangered animals' number one friend.

All over the globe, people are trying to repair the damage done to the environment and to the habitats of animals. Animal preserves are being set aside so that wild animals will have enough room to roam. Captive-breeding programs are under way for many endangered species. And laws are being written to make it illegal to buy or sell products coming from endangered animals.

How else can we protect endangered animals? Here are some things *you* can do to help.

1. *Do not buy products made from endangered animals.* Why? Because if no one buys them, then no one will be able to sell them! Prohibited items include anything made of ivory, fur, or other animal skins. But think about it, too, when you're shopping for a pet. Do you really want to buy a cool-looking parrot if the bird is endangered? The same goes for many exotic pets, including some lizards and tropical fish.

2. *Write letters to lawmakers who can influence laws*

*protecting wildlife.* You can start with your senators and representatives. Tell them that you care about endangered species and want the lawmakers to protect the habitats of these animals. You might also want to write to companies that do business in forests, oceans, and other natural areas. For instance, many paper companies are cutting down large forests. Some companies that catch tuna fish also catch dolphins in the same nets. And the dolphins die.

3. *Support your local zoo.* Many zoos are working hard to protect and breed endangered species. They also make a great effort to educate the public. When you volunteer your time or contribute money to a zoo, it's good for endangered animals everywhere. Many zoos have volunteer programs for students. Call the zoo and find out.

4. *Start a fund-raising project at school.* With the money you raise, you might be able to "adopt" an animal at a zoo or in a wildlife preserve. That means your class could help provide the money to feed and care for a beautiful whooping crane. Or a Komodo dragon!

5. *Be careful of your environment.* Think about how your actions might affect wildlife. For instance, when you need to throw away plastics, trash, or chemicals, be sure to put them in a proper container, and find out if they can be recycled. When you walk on the beach, be careful not to damage the plants growing on the sand dunes. And remember that many animals like their habitats just the way they are. When you visit a wilderness area, try to leave it exactly as you found it.

Most of all, wherever you go, remember the passenger pigeon. No matter how many there are of a particular animal, it can still become extinct. And extinct means gone *forever!*